COUNTRY LIFE

PICTURE BOOK OF BRITAIN

IN COLOUR

THE IMPOSING RUINS OF CORFE CASTLE, DORSET

COUNTRY LIFE

Picture Book of Britain

IN COLOUR

COUNTRY LIFE LTD LONDON

First published in 1957

Fifth impression 1966

© COUNTRY LIFE LIMITED

Tower House, Southampton St, W.C.2

Process engraving by

The Sun Engraving Co. Ltd, London and Watford

Printed in Great Britain by

Balding & Mansell Ltd, London and Wisbech

Bound by C. & H. T. Evans Ltd, Croydon

THE ILLUSTRATIONS

REFERENCE MAP
of
THE BRITISH ISLES

The numbers on the map are those
of the illustrations, and show the
approximate positions of the places
where the photographs were taken

LONDON DISTRICT

Each division on this border represents 2½ miles

Each division on this border represents 25 miles

Frontispiece

1. SPRING ON
LOCH TORRIDON

Looking across the blue waters of Loch Torridon, one gets a fine view of snow-capped Ben Alligin from a belt of conifers near Annat. This village is at the head of Upper Loch Torridon in Wester Ross, one of the most scenically beautiful regions in Scotland. Ben Alligin rises to a height of 3,232 feet on the north-east shore of the loch. Most of the hills in this neighbourhood are formed of the striking red sandstone called Torridon Sandstone, but Ben Alligin itself is formed of what is known as Hebridean Gneiss.

2. CANTERBURY CATHEDRAL

Canterbury, which the Romans knew as Durovernum and the Saxons as Cantwarabyrig, is the archiepiscopal see of the Primate of All England and one of the most historical cities in the country. After the murder of the Archbishop, Thomas à Becket, in 1170, it became a famous place of pilgrimage and it was to the shrine of 'the holy blissful martyr' that Chaucer's pilgrims were going in that April long ago. The present building was begun in the latter part of the twelfth century, replacing earlier ones that were totally destroyed by fire in 1067 and 1172. The Cathedral fortunately escaped destruction again, from German bombs, in 1942.

3. BOURTON-ON-THE-WATER

Spring in the Cotswolds. The low stone bridges crossing the river Windrush give rather a foreign air to this picture, yet nothing could really be more typically English than this charming Gloucestershire village. The river flows alongside the main street. The Cotswolds are a range of gentle limestone hills, extending over an area of about fifty miles lying mainly in Gloucestershire, but touching the neighbouring counties of Somerset, Oxfordshire and Worcestershire. In medieval times the Cotswolds were the centre of the woollen industry and were noted for their breed of sheep.

4. TRAFALGAR SQUARE

This photograph of one of London's most famous squares has something of the quality of a painting by Canaletto or Guardi. Nelson's Column, 184 feet in height and guarded at the base by Sir Edwin Landseer's celebrated lions, dominates the centre of the picture. Immediately behind is the National Gallery, the columns of whose portico originally formed part of Carlton House. On the right is the always well-attended church of St Martin-in-the-Fields, James Gibbs's masterpiece erected between 1721 and 1726. Behind may be seen the ball on top of the Coliseum.

5. LLYN GWYNANT, CAERNARVONSHIRE

This little lake, only about a mile long, lies to the south-east of the Snowdon range and four miles north-east of the village of Beddgelert. The Snowdon area contains a number of other equally charming little lakes, including Llyn Padarn, Llyn Peris, Llyn Quellyn and Llyn Llydaw. Snowdonia — a word that seems to have been invented by Thomas Pennant, the antiquarian author of *Tours of Wales*—has been designated as one of Britain's National Parks, thus helping to preserve its flora and fauna. From the Nant Gwynant valley came the Welsh Prince Madoc ab Owain Gwynedd, who is said to have discovered America centuries before Columbus.

6. THE 'BACKS', CAMBRIDGE

This fine study of the 'Backs' was taken in April, before the season when the waters of the Cam teem with punts and canoes. It was not until the eighteenth century that the colleges whose grounds adjoined the Cam began to take much interest in preserving the beauty of the 'Backs', which are now one of the most celebrated features of the university town. They run from Great Bridge down to the Mill Pool beyond Queens' College, passing a number of bridges, one of which — that of Trinity College — may be seen in this photograph.

⑦ WIDECOMBE-IN-THE-MOOR

Dartmoor in the spring can be very beautiful and many people who have gone there for holidays will recognize this picture of the Devonshire village of Widecombe-in-the-Moor, whose fine church has been called 'The Cathedral of Dartmoor'. Every September in Widecombe is held the fair, the journey to which proved too much for Tom Pearce's poor old grey mare, so that:

When the wind whistles cold on the moor of a night,
All along, down along, out along lee,
Tom Pearce's old mare doth appear gashly white,
Wi' Bill Brewer, Jan Stewer, Peter Gurney,
Peter Davy, Dan'l Whiddon, Harry Hawk,
Old Uncle Tom Cobleigh and all . . .

8. SNOWDON FROM LLYN LLYDAW

Two of the most popular routes up Snowdon start from Gorphwysfa, one running past Llyn Llydaw, which is crossed by a causeway, the other ascending by what is called the Pig Track. The more adventurous scorn such easy routes, of course, while the less energetic go up on the railway that has been running from Llanberis since 1896. Llyn Llydaw, a little over a mile in length, is surrounded on three sides by steep cliffs and is dominated at its head by the towering mass of Lliwedd (2,947 feet), the favourite Snowdon peak with rock climbers.

9. ST MAWES, CORNWALL

This attractive little town, with something of a Mediterranean atmosphere and setting, is situated on the promontory romantically named Roseland, opposite Falmouth, from which it is separated by three or four miles of sea. This photograph was taken in April before the season when the visitors begin flocking in. Considering that it is quite a small place, St Mawes has become a popular all-the-year-round resort, for in addition to its sheltered position, it is fortunate enough to have excellent hotels catering for even the most discriminating visitors.

10. BOLTON CASTLE, YORKSHIRE

There is something grim yet majestic about the well-preserved ruins of this famous Wensleydale castle, in the North Riding of Yorkshire. Lying about five miles north-west of Leyburn, it was built between 1378 and 1399. For hundreds of years it was a stronghold of the Scrope family, Wardens of the Western Marches. Mary, Queen of Scots, was imprisoned at Bolton from July, 1568 to January, 1569 and tradition has it that she tried unsuccessfully to escape from the castle. It ceased to be lived in after the Civil War.

11. LUDLOW, SHROPSHIRE

Above the bridge, crossing the river Teme, stands the famous border castle begun in the year 1086 and for many years the headquarters of the Lords President of the Marches. From this castle the young Prince Edward and his brother were removed by their uncle, Richard III, to become the 'Princes in the Tower'; here Prince Arthur, Henry VIII's elder brother, died shortly after his marriage to Catherine of Aragon; in the Great Hall Milton's *Comus* was performed for the first time in 1634; and here Samuel Butler worked on his *Hudibras* while he was steward to the Earl of Carbery.

12. BEDDGELERT, CAERNARVONSHIRE

As may be seen, this village in the Snowdon area has an extremely beautiful setting, where the little rivers Colwyn and Glaslyn meet. Its name is traditionally 'the grave of Gelert', the faithful — if legendary — hound which saved the infant son of Prince Llewelyn from a wolf and which was mistakenly slain by its master. The story, which has a number of variations, was first made popular in a poem by William Spencer in 1800; a year later the enterprising landlord of a local hotel erected 'Gelert's Grave' just outside the village.

⓭ WINDSOR CASTLE

This air photograph shows the superb setting — on a chalk cliff rising from the Thames — of the ancient fortress that has been a royal residence since the Norman conquest. The Round Tower in the centre dates from the reign of Henry II (1154–89). Behind it, to the left, are the State Apartments, with the Private Apartments and Visitors' Apartments slightly to the right, and the East Terrace Garden beyond. In front of the Round Tower is St George's Chapel, a superb example of English Gothic rivalling King's College Chapel, Cambridge. To the right of the Chapel are the apartments of the Military Knights of Windsor.

14. STRAND ON THE GREEN

For many years the north banks of the Thames have provided popular residential areas where many well-known men and women have lived. Chelsea, Hammersmith, Chiswick — all have their devotees; but many people consider that for picturesqueness and charm it is difficult to equal Strand on the Green, the street that runs for about half a mile along the river bank from Kew Bridge towards Chiswick Bridge. Many of the houses date from the eighteenth century and among the former residents was Zoffany, the painter, who used the local fishermen as his models.

15. THE MAWDDACH ESTUARY

There can be few gardens in the country that have such a superb natural setting as those at Glan-y-Mawddach, Merionethshire. They stand on the steep slopes of the north shore of the Mawddach Estuary, which extends from the seaside resort of Barmouth up to Dolgelly. From Glan-y-Mawddach there are magnificent views both up the estuary, as shown in this picture, and across it towards the Cader Idris range of mountains to the south. When Wordsworth visited Barmouth in 1824 he wrote of the 'sublime estuary', which compared, he said, with 'the finest of Scotland'.

16. CASTLE COMBE, WILTSHIRE

This is a real picture-book village, situated about five miles to the north-west of Chippenham, near the borders of Gloucestershire. It is full of delightful houses — a typical one of which is reflected in the water here — built of warm Cotswold stone. The Scrope family owned Castle Combe for hundreds of years, although at one time it was in the possession, through marriage, of Sir John Fastolf, the famous soldier, whose character and exploits were much maligned by Shakespeare in the person of Prince Hal's roisterous old friend, Sir John Falstaff.

17. THE HOUSES OF PARLIAMENT

This fine view, showing the whole length of the Houses of Parliament building, is taken from the south bank of the Thames. The Victoria Tower is on the left and the Clock Tower, from which 'Big Ben' sounds, on the right. The present building, designed by Sir Charles Barry, was erected between 1840 and 1850 to replace the previous premises which were almost totally destroyed by fire in 1834. During the last war the buildings were damaged on a number of occasions by bombs, the worst attack — in May, 1941 — almost completely destroying the Chamber of the House of Commons. This, and other damage, has now been made good again.

18. STRATFORD-ON-AVON

It is reckoned that some hundred thousand people visit Shakespeare's birthplace every year. This picture shows the Shakespeare Memorial Theatre in its beautiful setting on the banks of the river Avon. The architect was a woman, Elizabeth Scott, and it was opened in 1932, replacing the original theatre which was destroyed by fire in 1926. It is only in the last two hundred years that Stratford has, as it were, made a good thing out of its most famous son; in 1769 David Garrick arranged the first Shakespeare Jubilee there, since when the town has become a magnet for pilgrims from all over the world.

19. KERSEY, SUFFOLK

This very attractive and much-photographed village lies about ten miles west of Ipswich. In this picture we look down the main street, across the water-splash, up to the fine fourteenth-century church. In that century Suffolk became one of the richest counties in England because of the trade brought by exiled Flemish weavers; Kersey and the neighbouring village of Lindsey are said to have given their names to the once-popular woollen fabrics called 'Kersey' and 'Linsey-woolsey'.

20. YACHTING ON THE HOLY LOCH

The northern part of the Firth of Clyde and the lochs running into it are always popular centres for sailing. Here a small yacht is seen beating across the Holy Loch, on the Cowal Peninsula on the Argyllshire side of the Firth, north of Dunoon. Holy Loch is said to have derived its name from the fact that a ship was wrecked there carrying a load of earth from the Holy Land intended for the foundations of the Cathedral at Glasgow.

21. TORQUAY, DEVONSHIRE

From the air one sees how beautifully this famous resort is situated, sheltered by its surrounding hills. Yet only about a hundred and fifty years ago 'Tor Kay' consisted of a few fishermen's huts, with the little village of Tor (or Torre) a mile or so inland. The many boats in the inner and outer harbours show how popular Torquay is with yachtsmen. Torbay and its neighbourhood offer such ideal conditions for sailing that the yachting events in the 1948 Olympic Games were held there.

22. TENBY HARBOUR, PEMBROKESHIRE

Like Conway in Caernarvonshire, Tenby is one of the best existing examples of an old walled town; the walls, strengthened when the Spanish Armada was threatening the country, are still in good repair. Tenby was a flourishing seaport in Tudor times and had been well known both as a centre for the Flemish weavers and as a fishing port from the twelfth century, when Giraldus Cambrensis, the Welsh historian, was rector there. Nowadays the harbour, overlooked by the church, contains mainly pleasure craft.

23. STIRLING CASTLE

'The bulwark of the north, Grey Stirling' is one of the most historic towns in Scotland, its strategic position making it a key-place between the Highlands and the Lowlands. The castle, whose situation recalls that of Edinburgh, was a favourite residence of the Scottish Kings from the twelfth century. Both Alexander I and William the Lion died there; James II and James V were born there; Mary, Queen of Scots, was crowned there and her son, James I of England, spent his childhood there. From the castle walls can be seen the battlefield of Bannockburn.

24. THE BANN VALLEY, CO. DOWN

A typical piece of scenery on Northern Ireland's greatest river, near Hilltown, with the celebrated Mountains of Mourne in the background. The river Bann, which has a total length of about ninety miles, rises in the Mourne mountains and then descends quickly to Hilltown. Later it flows into Lough Neagh, passes along its whole length, and so out of it again, along the borders of Antrim and Londonderry, finally joining the sea at Port Stewart.

25. STONEHENGE, WILTSHIRE

Near Amesbury, on the edge of Salisbury Plain, stand these circles of towering stones, the most celebrated Neolithic and Bronze Age remains in the country. The origins of Stonehenge are shrouded in mystery, but it is fairly certain that it dates from between 2000 and 1400 B.C. The huge sarsen stones of the outer ring came from a site near Avebury, only a few miles away, but the 'blue' stones of spotted dolerite, in the inner circle, must have been brought from the Prescelly mountains in Pembrokeshire, probably by sea and then up the Avon from Christchurch — an extraordinary feat.

26. WARWICK CASTLE FROM THE AVON

The ancient county town of Warwick stands on the banks of the Avon and in this picture the river runs toward the mighty castle, which Sir Walter Scott called 'the fairest monument of ancient and chivalrous splendour which yet remains uninjured by time'. Its exterior is a fine example of a fourteenth-century fortress, while inside it is a sumptuous seventeenth-century dwelling. The great rooms in the medieval part of the building have been open to the public for something like a hundred and fifty years.

27. CLIFTON SUSPENSION BRIDGE

This air photograph gives a most striking and dramatic impression of the famous bridge spanning the Avon Gorge, linking the Gloucestershire portion of Bristol with that lying in Somerset. Suspended 245 feet above the river and measuring 702 feet in length, this world-famous bridge was designed by Isambard Kingdom Brunel, the younger of the two famous engineers. His plans for it were adopted in 1831, but owing to a shortage of funds, the bridge was not finally completed and opened until 1864, five years after his death.

28. PORTLOE, CORNWALL

Cornwall has for many years been a happy hunting ground for both artists and photographers; indeed, several places in Cornwall, including St Ives, Lamorna and the quaintly-named Mousehole, have become small artist colonies. Not only is the light in Cornwall often eminently suitable for painting, but the fishing villages, with their brightly painted boats drawn up in the harbour, provide excellent subjects for the artist. Portloe is a typical south Cornish village, situated on Veryan Bay, lying between Dodman Point and Nare Point.

29. PRINCES STREET, EDINBURGH

Looking down along the straight mile of one of the most famous streets in the world. Originally known as 'The Lang Gait', it was re-named in honour of the two eldest sons of George III, one of whom became George IV. On the left of the picture are the East Princes Street Gardens, beyond which are the buildings of the Royal Scottish Academy and the Scottish National Gallery, while beyond again are the West Princes Street Gardens. This photograph was taken from the Walter Scott Monument, and the two statues that may be seen in the first gardens are of John Wilson (Christopher North) and Dr Livingstone.

30. THE SUSSEX DOWNLAND

The narrow road runs towards a typical little village in this part of the Sussex Downs near Alfriston, lying only four or five miles inland from the sea. It was such scenes as this that inspired Rudyard Kipling, that great lover of Sussex, to write such lines as:

> *Here through the strong and shadeless days*
> *The twinkling silence thrills;*
> *Or little, lost, Down churches praise*
> *The Lord who made the hills.*

31. WATERLOO BRIDGE AND THE THAMES

This is London's newest — and, many people think, finest — bridge, connecting the Strand on the north side of the Thames with the area round Waterloo Station on the south side. Designed by Sir Giles Gilbert Scott, it was officially opened in 1945 and replaced the earlier bridge built by Sir John Rennie between 1811 and 1817. This bridge had shown signs of weakening in 1923 and began to be demolished about ten years later. Beyond Waterloo Bridge can be seen Blackfriars Bridge, while to the left runs the Victoria Embankment.

32. ST EDMUND HALL, OXFORD

This is the last survivor of Oxford's many medieval Halls, which were kind of residential hostels for undergraduates, all of which except this one either disappeared or were absorbed into the various colleges. Founded in the thirteenth century and named after St Edmund of Abingdon, the Archbishop of Canterbury who taught at Oxford between 1195 and 1200, its gracious quadrangle, seen in this photograph, dates from the middle of the seventeenth century.

33. VENTNOR,
ISLE OF WIGHT

The Isle of Wight is about twenty-three miles long by thirteen miles wide and Ventnor is in the extreme south. Its situation — on a series of narrow terraces above the sea and under the steep edge of St Boniface Down, the highest point in the island — gives it something of the air of a town on the French or Italian Rivieras. With its mild climate that Dickens indeed found too hot, Ventnor is one of the most popular resorts in an island that is itself almost one large holiday resort.

34. CUL MOR
FROM STACK POLLY

From the summit pinnacles of Stack Polly (2,009 feet) one can look across the blue waters of Loch Lurgain to the peaks of Cul Mor (2,786 feet). This north-west corner of Ross and Cromarty and neighbouring Sutherland are particularly rich in striking mountain peaks —others being Coulbeg (2,523 feet), Suilven (2,399 feet) sometimes known as the Sugar Loaf, and Canisp (2,779 feet) — that are beloved of all rock climbers.

35. BOURNEMOUTH FROM THE AIR

This is the famous Hampshire resort that was described — under the name of 'Sandbourne' — by Thomas Hardy in *Tess of the D'Urbervilles* as 'a Mediterranean lounging-place on the English Channel'. Bournemouth has grown from a small fishing village in the last hundred and fifty years, helped by the fact that its sheltered situation and pine-scented air made it an extremely healthy place. Robert Louis Stevenson lived there for his health between 1884 and 1887, just before sailing to the South Seas for the last time.

36. OFF LAND'S END

In spite of the crowds of visitors which one is apt to encounter there, the granite rocks of Land's End, rising sixty feet out of the sea, always have an air of romance about them. For this is the most westerly point of England, formerly known to the Cornish people as Penwith. Beyond Land's End may be seen the famous Longships Lighthouse; there has been a lighthouse on this rocky site since the end of the eighteenth century.

37. LORD LEYCESTER'S HOSPITAL, WARWICK

Dating from the fourteenth century, this beautiful old building, near the West Gate of Warwick, was made into a hospital or almshouse for 'twelve poor brethren' by Queen Elizabeth's favourite, Robert Dudley, Earl of Leicester, in 1571. Among the relics kept there is a piece of needlework said to have been sewed by the Earl's ill-fated wife, Amy Robsart, whose story Walter Scott told in *Kenilworth*. The heraldic crests on the walls date from Elizabethan times. The 'brethren' are old soldiers.

38. PORTSCATHO, CORNWALL

On the other side of the Roseland Peninsula from St Mawes is this delightful fishing village. It is situated on Gerrans Bay, which stretches from Roseland to Nare Point. The climate of south Cornwall is normally more kindly and temperate than in any other part of England, and this particular part of the county — Portloe, which can be seen in Plate 28, is another place in this immediate neighbourhood — is always a popular centre for both residents and holiday-makers.

39. RYDAL WATER, WESTMORLAND

This charming little lake — only about three quarters of a mile long and a quarter of a mile wide, and connecting with its larger neighbours, Grasmere and Windermere, by the river Rothay — lies a few miles to the north-west of Ambleside. At the east end of Rydal Water, in the house called Rydal Mount, Wordsworth lived from 1813 until his death in 1850, while nearby at Nab Cottage lived De Quincey in 1816 and Hartley Coleridge from 1840 to 1849.

40. LINCOLN CATHEDRAL

This picture shows the famous West Front of the cathedral, one of the finest in the country. The centre point and the lower part of the towers — St Mary's Tower on the left and St Hugh's on the right — survive from Norman times, but most of the building dates from the thirteenth century. St Hugh, after whom the tower is named, was Bishop Hugh of Avalon, under whom the cathedral was re-built and extended after the original Norman building was badly damaged by an earthquake in 1185.

41. ON THE CIOCH, ISLE OF SKYE

A group of climbers are here seen perched on the curiously shaped rock pinnacle called the Cioch, looking across Glen Brittle towards the Outer Hebrides. It juts out from the north-facing cliffs of Sron na Ciche, a subsidiary range of the Western Cuillin running west-south-west from Sgurr Alasdair, the highest point of the Cuillin. The Cioch, first climbed in 1906, has been called 'the Mecca of British cragsmen' and many famous climbs lead up the face of Sron na Ciche to and from the Cioch, which is itself about 2,300 feet above sea level.

42. WINCHESTER, HAMPSHIRE

As may be seen in this photograph taken from the air, the mighty cathedral — at 556 feet it is the longest in England, the nave alone measuring 351 feet — dominates the ancient and historic town. The Britons knew Winchester as Caer Gwent and the Romans as Venta Belgarum; it was the capital city of Alfred the Great and many of his successors, including Canute; Edward the Confessor was crowned there and William the Conqueror, who made Winchester a joint capital with London, took the precaution to be crowned in both places, an example followed by several other kings.

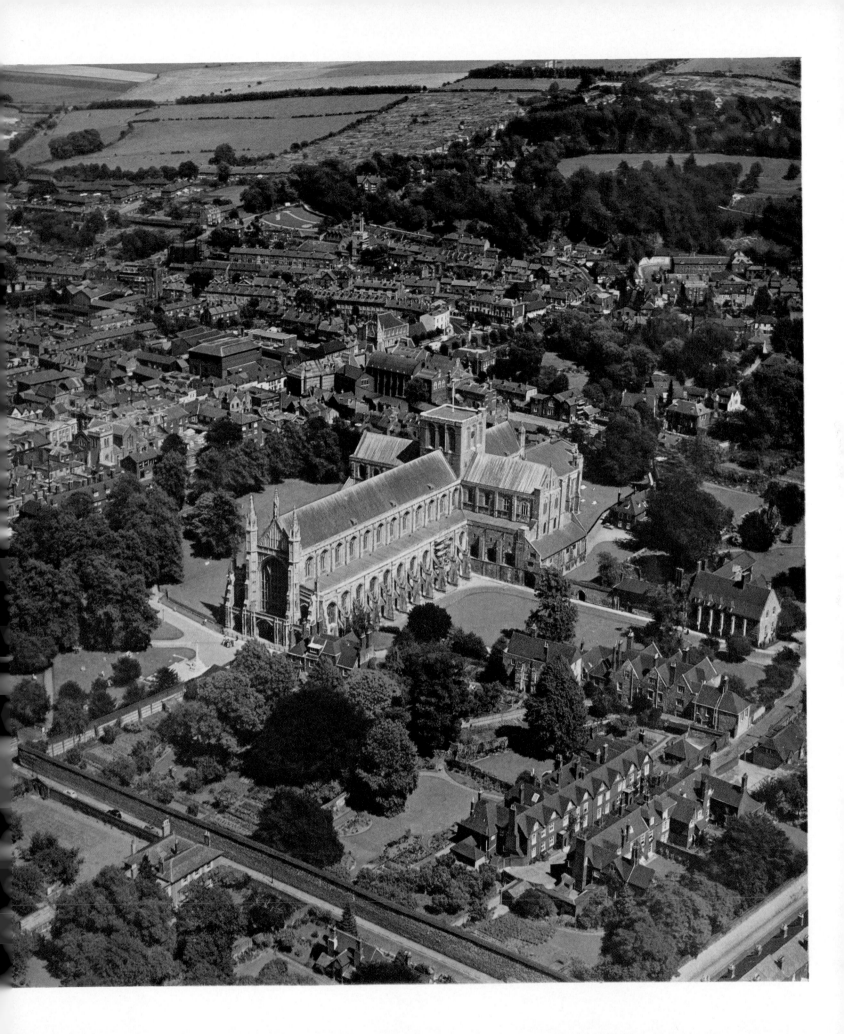

43. STANTON, GLOUCESTERSHIRE

Some twelve miles north-west of Bourton-on-the-Water, which may be seen in Plate 3, and almost in Worcestershire, is this other charming village built of mellow Cotswold stone. Almost every house has its garden plot, gay with flowers, and in the centre of the village is the ancient stone cross whose base possibly dates from the twelfth century. It was at Stanton, when staying with the rector who had been his pupil at Oxford, that John Wesley fell in love with the rector's sister — although in the end the romance came to nothing.

44. DERWENTWATER, CUMBERLAND

Many people consider that Derwentwater is the most scenically perfect of all the British lakes. Lying in Borrowdale, just to the south of Keswick, it is three miles long and about a mile wide. Derwentwater is not only beautiful in itself, but on account of its majestic and mountainous surrounding scenery, with Skiddaw dominating it to the north. In the lake itself are several quite sizable islands, including one on which Lord Derwentwater appropriately had a house and another, St Hubert's Isle, where a disciple of St Cuthbert lived in the seventh century.

45. CHILHAM, KENT

Half-timbered cottages, whitewash and the imposing church tower give variety to the scene in this typical mid-Kent village. It lies a little over five miles south-west of Canterbury, where the valley of the river Stour crosses the North Downs. Chilham has associations with the United States, for here was born Edward Digges, the Puritan Governor of Virginia between 1655 and 1657, whose family owned the manor and who, being ardent Royalists, could not have been too proud of young Edward. Another seventeenth-century Governor, Lord Culpeper, came from nearby Leeds Castle.

46. HELVELLYN AND FAIRFIELD

The Lake District mountains may not be very exciting for the expert climber, but they are extremely beautiful to look at. Helvellyn (3,118 feet) is the third highest peak in England (after Scafell and Scafell Pike), while its more modest neighbour, Fairfield, is a mere 2,863 feet. Helvellyn is well worth climbing, for from the summit one can see every other important Lake District peak; Windermere, Coniston and Ullswater; Morecambe Bay, the Solway Firth and the hills of Dumfriesshire.

47. TOWER BRIDGE

The twin bascules or drawbridges have been raised to allow the passage of a ship too large to pass underneath; although each bascule weighs about a thousand tons, they can be raised by hydraulic machinery in a minute and a half. The actual bridge is about 800 feet long and its fine lines, someone once said, are spoiled by 'the lace flounces of prettified Scotch baronical architecture'. It was built between 1886 and 1894 to the design of Sir Horace Jones and Sir John Wolfe Barry. Tower Bridge lies immediately below the Tower of London.

48. SALISBURY CATHEDRAL

The cathedral is not only beautiful itself, but has a beautiful setting when seen, as it is here, rising above the quiet waters of the river Avon. The building is unique among English cathedrals in that it is almost entirely of one period, the thirteenth century; the celebrated spire is, at 404 feet, the loftiest in England. An old local rhyme says that the cathedral has as many pillars, windows and doors as the year has hours, days and months! Salisbury, which Thomas Hardy wrote of as 'Melchester' in his Wessex novels, is the county town of Wiltshire.

49. AUTUMN
ON LOCH RANNOCH

Beyond the tranquil waters of this long, narrow loch — it is about ten miles long, but not more than one mile wide — can be seen the graceful quartzite cone of Schiehallion. Rising to 3,547 feet, Schiehallion dominates this part of northern Perthshire. It is not difficult to climb and in the eighteenth century was used by Nevil Maskelyne, the Astronomer Royal, in his experiments relating to the specific gravity and weight of the earth and into the scientific attraction of mountains; most modern visitors, however, will be content to enjoy the scenery.

50. WELLS CATHEDRAL, SOMERSET

In this photograph, taken on a fine autumn day, the small but exquisite cathedral is seen from the gardens of the Bishop's Palace, reflected in the still waters of the moat. Parts of the cathedral date from the late twelfth century, while the largely unspoilt North Porch was built about 1213 by Bishop Jocelin, who was also responsible for the famous West Front — containing the finest collection of medieval ecclesiastical sculpture in the country — and the Palace. The moat dates from about a century later and in the gardens is a fifteenth-century well house.

51. LOOKING ACROSS ULLSWATER

Many people find the Lake District at its most enchanting in the autumn and this picture of Ullswater provides one reason; it vividly recalls the description of Ullswater that Wordsworth wrote in his *Guide to the Lakes* after visiting it at this season of the year. After Windermere, Ullswater (seven and a half miles long by three quarters of a mile wide) is the largest of the English lakes and it forms part of the boundary between the counties of Cumberland and Westmorland.

52. KING'S COLLEGE CHAPEL, CAMBRIDGE

This pictorial record of Beautiful Britain is appropriately brought to an end with this charming study of the boys of King's College choir school, in their silk hats, walking across the snow to attend morning service in the chapel. This sublime building was begun during the Wars of the Roses in the reign of the unhappy Henry VI, who was also the founder of the college, and finished in the more peaceful reign of Henry VII. It moved Wordsworth to write in a sonnet, after a visit to Cambridge:

> *They dreamt not of a perishable home*
> *Who thus could build. Be mine, in hours of fear*
> *Or grovelling thought, to seek a refuge here.*

THE SECOND

COUNTRY LIFE

PICTURE BOOK OF BRITAIN

IN COLOUR

THE VILLAGE OF THORNTON DALE IN THE NORTH RIDING OF YORKSHIRE

THE ILLUSTRATIONS

REFERENCE MAP
of
THE BRITISH ISLES

The numbers on the map are those
of the illustrations, and show the
approximate positions of the places
where the photographs were taken

LONDON DISTRICT

Each division on this border represents 2½ miles

Each division on this border represents 25 miles

① ST JAMES'S PARK

This picture was taken on a fine summer evening in St James's Park — a park well known and loved by Londoners for its fine flower beds, its beautiful lake and the variety of waterfowl which make their home there. The Park, which stretches from Horse Guards Parade (the Foreign Office building can be seen in the background) to Buckingham Gate, and is bordered by The Mall and Bird Cage Walk, was part of an area of about 100 acres bought by Henry VIII from the Abbot of Westminster. It was first opened to the public, however, in the reign of Charles II, who took a great interest in its lay-out and often strolled there, looking at the waterfowl that were in the Park even in his day.

2. SUNSET OVER THE THAMES

Discovery, built for the Antarctic expedition of 1901–4 and commanded by Captain R. F. Scott, makes a fine picture in the setting sun. It is moored in the river off the Embankment and is now used as a training ship for Sea Scouts. The Victoria Embankment extends from Westminster Bridge along the north bank of the Thames to Blackfriars Bridge, a magnificent curve of nearly a mile and a half. In the background is Waterloo Bridge, leading south to the Festival Hall and Waterloo Station, and on the right of *Discovery* is the silhouette of Shell Mex House. The middle sky-line shows buildings in Northumberland Avenue.

3. IN THE EMBANKMENT GARDENS

This long, narrow garden, sandwiched between the Thames Embankment and the cliff-like buildings of Adelphi Terrace, is gay with flowers from spring to autumn and contains many fine trees. This is a favourite lunch hour retreat for those who work in the neighbourhood of the Strand and one which is of particular interest to gardeners. In this picture the famous clock on Shell Mex House can be seen — it is the largest clock in London, the dial being 25 ft. in diameter. At the Hungerford Bridge end of the Gardens is York Gate, the water gate of the former York House, designed by Inigo Jones and erected in 1626. Its present situation reminds us of the one-time course of the river before the construction of the Embankment (1864–70). There are several monuments in the Gardens, including a statue of Robert Burns, a memorial to the Imperial Camel Corps and a bust of Sir Arthur Sullivan.

4. ROSES IN REGENT'S PARK

This splendid park, 541 acres in extent, and only a mile or so from Oxford Circus, contains many magnificent features, including herbaceous borders, a rock and water garden, elaborate bedding schemes, and an extensive lake for sailing and boating. There is, however, nothing more popular or beautiful than Queen Mary's Rose Garden, in which many thousands of roses bloom with a freedom not exceeded in any country garden. In the summer the Open Air Theatre — near the Rose Garden — attracts many visitors, and on Easter and Whit Mondays parades of cart horses and van horses are held in the Park. The Park derives its name from the Prince Regent (afterwards George IV), for whom it was designed in 1812, by John Nash.

5. DAFFODILS
NEAR LESNES ABBEY

Looking at this lovely springtime picture one gets the impression of being in the heart of the country. These woods are, in fact, on the very edge of London at Erith, once a place of maritime importance on the Thames and a resort of Londoners, but now the centre of numerous industries, mainly engineering, with Woolwich Arsenal close by. As may be expected from its connection with the early history of England, Kent possesses a larger than average number of monastic foundations. At Abbey Wood, to the west of Erith, are the remains of Lesnes (sometimes spelt Lessness) Abbey, which was founded in 1178 and belonged to the Augustinian canons.

6. HEVER CASTLE, KENT

Kent is rich in historic buildings. Among the numerous medieval and renaissance houses in the county, the most important are Ightham Mote, Penshurst, Knole, Hever and Leeds Castles. Hever Castle, once the seat of the Boleyns and the scene of the courtship of Anne Boleyn by Henry VIII, is now maintained by the Astor family. It was the first Lord Astor who made the marvellous eighteen-acre lake and the Italian gardens. Hever is two miles south-east of Edenbridge and is entered from a lane that goes round the Boleyn Arms and the church. The River Eden flows by Hever and Chiddingstone and joins the Medway at Penshurst. The moat is pictured here, the banks of which are planted with daffodils.

⑦ ACROSS ROMNEY MARSH

Romney Marsh, in the southernmost corner of Kent, is more or less crescent-shaped, full of ditches and channels and consequently extremely rich in pasture for sheep and cattle. We owe this marshland, which comprises 45,000 acres, to the Romans, who built the sea wall at Dymchurch for reclaiming land from the sea. It extends north of Romney, one of the Cinque Ports, a small town now more than a mile from the sea. The many Martello towers, which border the Marsh to seaward, are relics of the Napoleonic invasion which never came off. Of the five Romney churches mentioned in the Domesday Survey, only one remains — a rich Norman building dedicated to St Nicholas.

8. THE SEVEN SISTERS, NEAR EASTBOURNE

The Seven Sisters, some of which are shown here, make a striking picture and form some of the finest coastal scenery in the country. They lie to the west of Beachy Head, that magnificent headland near Eastbourne, where the South Downs reach the sea and end in a sheer precipice of chalk cliffs 536 ft. in height. The Sisters, situated between Birling Gap and Cuckmere Haven, have each got a name and, beginning from the Birling Gap end, they are called : Went Hill Brow, Baily's Hill, Flagstaff Point, Bran Point, Rough Brow, Short Brow, and Haven Brow. Much of this area is National Trust property. From Eastbourne to Birling Gap it is five and a quarter miles on foot.

9. COWDRAY PARK, SUSSEX

The setting sun gives a wonderful flame-coloured glow to the rushes and trees on Benbow Pond in Cowdray Park, Lord Cowdray's seat near Midhurst. Note the three-quarter moon in the eastern sky. In this beautiful park, with its many splendid beeches, oaks and Spanish chestnuts, may be seen the magnificent ruins of Cowdray, one of the most imposing Tudor mansions in Sussex. A curse of destruction by fire and water is said to have been laid on Cowdray and its owners, for in 1793 the house was destroyed by fire and three members of the family in the line of succession died by drowning.

10. ARUNDEL CASTLE FROM THE AIR

This fine view from the air shows the magnificent Arundel Castle, seat of the Duke of Norfolk. The castle — on a site that had been a stronghold of the Romans and Saxons — dominates the small market town, set on a hill-side above the Arun, and the flat coastal plain below it. The 'honour' of Arundel was conferred by William the Conqueror on Roger de Montgomery, first Earl of Shrewsbury and Arundel, who was a commander at the battle of Hastings. The Earl began the present castle in 1086, the greater part of which was destroyed in the seventeenth century, but almost completely reconstructed at the end of the nineteenth century by the father of the present Duke. The Norman keep, barbican and drawbridge still remain.

11. PRIMROSE PATH: NEAR COWFOLD

This woodland track immediately calls to mind Shakespeare's lines about ' the primrose path of dalliance ', along which anyone would be glad to tread, ' puff'd and reckless libertine ' or not. Cowfold is a pleasant village in the West Sussex weald, about six miles south-east of Horsham. Its church has the famous 10 ft. long brass to Thomas Neldon (d. 1433), prior of Lewes, which is said to be the finest in the county and one of the most notable in England. At Parkminster, one and a half miles south, is the Carthusian monastery of St Hugh of Lincoln.

12. ON THE WEY,
NEAR GUILDFORD

In this picture the glorious, orange-coloured tints of the autumn leaves are reflected in the tranquil waters of the River Wey as it runs near Guildford. The Wey, which rises near Alton, in Hampshire, becomes navigable at Godalming and, just before reaching Guildford, is joined by the Tillingbourne. After leaving Guildford, the Wey flows past Woking and eventually joins the Thames at Weybridge. In its course of approximately thirty-five miles it is crossed by a number of very ancient bridges, some dating back to medieval times; two that are particularly worth visiting are the thirteenth-century structures at Eashing, about four miles south-west of Guildford.

13. SHERE, SURREY

Shere is one of several beautiful Surrey villages in the well-wooded valley of the Tillingbourne, between Dorking and Guildford. These delightful, creeper-covered, sixteenth-seventeenth century cottages, some of half-timbered construction, line the main street. Shere was once noted for its weavers — while the name of the neighbouring village of Abinger Hammer is a reminder of the days when ironfounding was a flourishing industry in Surrey. The church at Shere has a Norman tower and doorway to the south aisle and an unusual thirteenth century font of Purbeck marble.

14. REIGATE HILL WOODS

These lovely woods on Surrey's Reigate Hill — seen here in early spring — form part of a large area of beechwood, copse and open down on the summit and escarpment of the North Downs; they are now under the protection of the National Trust. The old market town of Reigate is situated at the foot of the Downs and retains several attractive old houses. Reigate Castle, around which in Norman times the town flourished, has now been demolished, its site being used as public gardens. The first mention of the name Reigate (possibly the ' gate of the roe-deer ') occurs in 1170 — before that the place was known as Cherchefelle, or Churchfield.

15. IN KEW GARDENS

The Royal Botanic Gardens of Kew date back to 1759 when the Dowager Princess Augusta, mother of George III, laid out a private botanic garden in the grounds of her mansion, Kew House. The gardens, which now extend over nearly 300 acres, were adopted as a national establishment in 1840 and are a constant source of pleasure to the thousands of visitors who go to see the magnificent collection of trees and plants. The museums and hothouses (especially the Palm House), the lofty pagoda (erected in 1761) and the flagstaff (159 ft. high) made of a single trunk of a Douglas pine, all claim a considerable amount of attention. Our picture shows the pond opposite the Palm House, with one of the museum buildings beyond. The name Kew first occurs in Henry VII's time, when it was spelt Kayhough (' quay on the Hoe ').

16. BURNHAM BEECHES

This beautiful and justly popular area of Buckinghamshire was originally part of an ancient forest and some of the pollarded trees — they look as though they had inspired Arthur Rackham's fantastic drawings — are thought to be upwards of a thousand years old. The woods formerly belonged to Burnham Abbey and after the Dissolution of the monasteries they remained private property until 1897, when the Corporation of London bought the 450 acres that are now open to the public. Every year Burnham Beeches are visited by thousands of Londoners.

17. BRAY LOCK, BERKSHIRE

The charming village of Bray lies on the Thames between Windsor and Maidenhead. In fine weather during the summer months it is almost too popular, hundreds of people visiting it on Saturdays and Sundays by river or road. Bray has several times won the prize for the best-kept lock garden on the Thames and visitors can see, in the trim lawns, beds filled with flowers of many kinds. Bray was the parish of the famous opportunist parson who, in the old rhyme, said:

And this is law that I'll maintain
Until my dying day, sir,
That whatsoever king shall reign,
Still I'll be Vicar of Bray, sir.

18. CHRISTCHURCH, HAMPSHIRE

Christchurch, which lies in the south-west of Hampshire, just along the coast to the east of Bournemouth, was mentioned in Saxon documents under the name of Tweotneam or Tweotnaeteam (roughly translated as ' the town on two rivers '); this name long survived as Christchurch Twineham. The two rivers — the Avon and the Stour — are a constant source of enjoyment to the local boatmen and fishermen ; indeed the salmon fishing here is extremely valuable. Beyond the two fishermen in this picture, sitting comfortably in their boat, can be seen the magnificent Augustinian priory church of Holy Trinity, from which the town derives its present name. Part of the building is Norman and it is the longest parish church in England, measuring 312 ft. in length. Inside is a monument to Shelley and many others of interest.

19. H.M.S. VICTORY
AT PORTSMOUTH

Portsmouth has been famous as a naval dockyard since the time of Henry VIII. Captain Bligh sailed from Portsmouth in the *Bounty ;* Lord Anson landed there after his voyage round the world ; and almost every famous British sailor has had some connection with ' Pompey '. Nelson spent his last night in England there and his body was brought back to Portsmouth after the battle of Trafalgar. His flagship, *Victory,* lies in front of the entrance of the Old (or King Charles's) Dock and has been restored and fitted out much as she was at Trafalgar. *Victory* still flies the flag of the Commander-in-Chief, Portsmouth.

20. CASTLE COMBE, WILTSHIRE

This village, in the extreme north-west of Wiltshire, where it adjoins Gloucestershire, looks beautiful at any season of the year ; but snow on the roofs of the old, mellow Cotswold-stone houses seems to give an added beauty. Everything in and around the village — cottages, church, inns, market cross, ancient manor house — combines to make a harmonious and picturesque whole. The Norman castle, which gave the village its name, has long vanished, but the Norman family of Scrope remained lords of the manor here for five hundred years until the latter part of the nineteenth century.

21. THE HENLEY REGATTA COURSE

The world-famous Henley Regatta has been held annually, except during the two World Wars, since 1839. It is the chief British rowing meeting and became a ' Royal ' event as long ago as 1851. It has perhaps lost some of its social elegance since those Victorian and Edwardian summers, but it still attracts oarsmen from all over the world ; Russian crews have often taken part in recent years — very successfully, too. The Grand Challenge Cup, the Silver Goblets and the Diamond Sculls are among the famous trophies competed for. Henley itself is one of the oldest towns in Oxfordshire, dating from Roman times.

22. OXFORD FROM THE AIR

In the centre of the foreground in this striking aerial photograph of Oxford may be seen the famous 'Tom Quad' of Christ Church, with Peckwater Quad to the left and the spire of the Cathedral to the right. The tower of Merton College is in the middle of the picture, with Magdalen Tower framed by the dark green trees. 'Tom Quad' measures 264 ft. by 261 ft. and is the largest of the Oxford college quadrangles, while Christ Church itself — familiarly known as 'The House' (*Aedes Christi*) — is the largest of Oxford's colleges. It owes its original foundation to Cardinal Wolsey, who named it Cardinal College ; after his fall, the college was renamed by Henry VIII.

23. THE SHAKESPEARE MEMORIAL THEATRE

In this striking picture the sun causes the Memorial theatre to have an almost orange reflection in the waters of the River Avon. The original theatre, built between 1877 and 1879, and where Sir Frank Benson produced all Shakespeare's plays except *Titus Andronicus*, was destroyed by fire in 1926. The present building, designed by a woman architect, Elisabeth Whitworth Scott, was opened in 1932. Visitors now come to Stratford-on-Avon in their thousands for the two annual seasons of plays and to see the various local places associated with Shakespeare.

24. WORCESTER
FROM THE AIR

The cathedral, beautifully sited on the banks of the river Severn, dominates this picture of the city from the air. Beyond it are the Severn Bridge, connecting Bridge Street and New Road, and the railway viaduct. To the left is the Worcestershire county cricket ground, at which it is customary for visiting Test teams to play their first county match. Worcester has been an episcopal see since the year 680 and the present cruciform cathedral, dedicated to Christ and St Mary the Virgin, consists of structures of a variety of periods, including a Norman crypt.

25. DOVECOT AT LUNTLEY COURT, HEREFORDSHIRE

This well-preserved four-gabled dovecot dates from the middle of the seventeenth century and is said to contain over five hundred nesting places. In those days in country houses pigeons were often kept as a welcome addition to the menu ; Herefordshire is particularly rich in such interesting old structures. In the background may be seen Luntley Court itself, a splendid example of small, black-and-white, timber-fronted manor-house, bearing the date 1674. It stands to the west of the village of Dilwyn, about five and a half miles south-west of Leominster, on the road to Weobley.

26. SNOWSHILL, GLOUCESTERSHIRE

These tiny cottages, built in the warm stone of the Cotswold country, make a charming picture with their gay gardens of tulips and wallflowers. Snowshill is a small village in the north-east corner of Gloucestershire — a county distinctly divided into three main sections ; to the east the Cotswold hills, to the west the Vale overlooking the rich valley of the Severn, and the beautiful and historic Forest of Dean, which lies between the Wye and the Severn. The font in the church, which can be seen just beyond the cottages, is fifteenth century, but the church itself is a comparatively modern building.

27. THE GAMEKEEPER, ORCHARDLEIGH

There is something essentially English about this winter scene in Somerset, showing the gamekeeper, with his gun, leaning on the gate, attended by his two dogs. Orchardleigh, which is a hamlet about two miles north of Frome, was the 'Gardenleigh' of Sir Henry Newbolt's historical novel, *The Old Country*, in which the chief characters live in both the twentieth and the fourteenth centuries. Newbolt was married to Margaret, daughter of the Rev. William Arthur Duckworth, of Orchardleigh, and he is buried in the churchyard of the little church that stands on a unique island site in a lake.

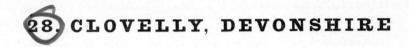 28. CLOVELLY, DEVONSHIRE

This delightful little fishing village set in a rocky cleft eleven miles south-west of Bideford has for long been a popular holiday resort. Clovelly consists of a cluster of old-fashioned houses, sheltered on three sides by thick woods. Its cobbled main street descends 400 ft. to the pier. This photograph of fishing nets drying in the sun reminds us of the scene that occurred so often in Charles Kingsley's boyhood. His father, the rector, used to hold services at the harbour when the herring-boats put to sea. Perhaps it was during one of these services that Charles Kingsley conceived the idea of his historical novel, *Westward Ho!*

29. BURRATOR RESERVOIR, DARTMOOR

Bluebells are out near this corner of the picturesque and, in places, lake-like reservoir that supplies the Plymouth district with water. It is situated about two miles to the east of Yelverton, on the south-west corner of Dartmoor. Rising beyond the water and the trees that are part of one of the local afforestation schemes are the striking rocks of Sheepstor. In the churchyard of the village of Sheepstor are buried Sir James Brooke, the man who made himself Rajah of Sarawak, in the north-west of Borneo, and his nephew, Sir Charles Brooke, the second Rajah. They came of an old Devonshire family.

30. ST IVES, CORNWALL

The church right down in the harbour is dedicated to St Ia, a fifth century Irish saint who came over to Cornwall and who gave her name to the town. The church itself dates from the early part of the fifteenth century and has some fine bench-ends. Now a popular holiday resort, St Ives has a long history; Perkin Warbeck, pretender to the throne in the reign of Henry VII, landed there from Ireland to begin his abortive rebellion that brought him to the scaffold. St Ives has been a favourite place with artists since the days in the last century when Whistler and his pupil, Sickert, founded an artists' colony there.

31. COVERACK HARBOUR

Coverack is one of several small fishing villages, justly popular with holiday-makers, on the Lizard peninsula, in south Cornwall. There are fine bathing beaches near at hand and the many gaily-coloured boats in the harbour give some indication of the way in which visitors like to spend at least part of their holiday. Coverack is a lifeboat station, and one realises the reason when one remembers that just off the coast is the dangerous reef called The Manacles, on which many ships, bound for Falmouth, were wrecked in the old days. In the churchyard at neighbouring St Keverne are buried some four hundred drowned people.

32. HODNET HALL, SHROPSHIRE

Hodnet Hall is situated five-and-a-half miles south-west of Market Drayton. The house, a large neo-Elizabethan structure of the mid-nineteenth century, is an interesting example of Victorian imitation; and the contents are superb. But the Hall is famous chiefly for its garden, the work of the late Brigadier A. G. W. Heber Percy. From 1926 until his death in 1962 he had annually planted something between 600 and 800 shrubs and trees, resulting in a magnificent and varied collection arranged in a bold and coherent design. The house and garden are owned by Brigadier Heber Percy's Trustees and are open to the public in the summer.

33. IN THE GANLLWYD VALLEY

The Ganllwyd Valley, one of the most striking in North Wales, runs northwards from Dolgelley, towards Trawsfynydd and its lake-reservoir. Several small rivers flow through the valley and in the glen of the river Gamlam is a spectacular waterfall called Rhaiadr Ddu, easily reached from the village of Ganllwyd or the inn at Tyn-y-groes, a favourite resort of the many anglers who come to this part of Merionethshire. A great deal of the locality, comprising the Dolmelynllyn estate of 1,249 acres, is fortunately preserved by the National Trust.

34. HARLECH CASTLE

Harlech, in Merionethshire, is not only one of the most romantically situated of Welsh castles, but one of the most historic. It
was built between 1283 and 1289 as an important link in
Edward I's chain of fortresses. It was besieged many times,
notably by Madoc ap Llewelyn soon after it was erected, by the
great Owen Glendower in 1404 and by the Yorkists in the Wars
of the Roses in 1468, when the siege is said to have inspired the
famous song about the ' men of Harlech '. During the Civil
War it was the last Welsh castle to fall to the Roundheads.
The view from the battlements is breath-taking.

35. THE RIVER LLUGWY, CAERNARVONSHIRE

The valley of the Llugwy contains some of the grandest scenery in North Wales ; here it is seen in the autumn, with the leaves giving an added warmth to the colouring. The river rises on the peak called Glyder-fawr (3,279 ft.), one of the twin peaks of the range usually called The Glyders — the other being Glyder-fach (3,262 ft.). From there it flows south-east for about ten miles through the valley and eventually joins the river Conway at Bettws-y-Coed. This is the most convenient place to stay for exploring the Llugwy valley.

36. IN THE OGWEN VALLEY

Like the previous picture, this photograph gives some idea of the scenery to be found in the district loosely called Snowdonia. The river Ogwen issues from Llyn Ogwen, about five miles south-east of Bethesda, Caernarvonshire, and flows north-west for some ten miles, eventually coming out into the Menai Strait near Penrhyn Castle, opposite Anglesey. The Ogwen more or less follows the course of the famous Nant Ffrancon pass, which runs roughly parallel with, and to the north-east of, the other famous Snowdon pass of Llanberis.

37. A COLOURFUL LANGDALE GARDEN

Birches and heather give colour to this garden in the Great Langdale Valley, in the heart of the Lake District National Park. The peak in the background is Harrison Stickle (2,401 ft.), the higher of the two Langdale Pikes, the other being Pike o' Stickle (2,323 ft.). The district is much favoured by walkers and climbers who delight in the natural beauty of this small mountain sanctuary. The Park extends roughly from Caldbeck (John Peel's village) in the north to Newby Bridge in the south, and from Ennerdale Water in the west to Haweswater in the east.

38. DERWENTWATER

Derwentwater is claimed by many to be the most beautiful of all the lakes in England. For this lake, three miles long and one mile wide, is surrounded by rich scenery, a wonderful blending of crag, green fell and wooded slopes, with an imposing background of mountains — and added to this a final charm is lent by the trim wooded islets dotting its surface. The larger islands are Derwent Isle, which is privately owned, Lord's Island, now National Trust property, and St Herbert's Island, where Herebert, a disciple of St Cuthbert, lived in the seventh century.

39. LOCH INCH, STRANRAER

Loch Inch, one of Scotland's most famous gardens, is ideally situated on a narrow stretch of land between White and Black Lochs. The garden was originally laid out by Field Marshal the 2nd Earl of Stair, between 1733 and 1742. It was neglected after his death, but towards the end of the nineteenth century the 10th Earl restored and enlarged it. A great variety of trees and shrubs now thrive in this garden in Wigtownshire on the west coast of Scotland, which has as its central feature the ruins of the old castle. The rhododendrons are pictured here in the more formal setting of the house.

40. GOAT FELL
SEEN FROM BRODICK

This picture was taken from the jetty, looking across Brodick bay towards Goat Fell (2,866 ft.), Walter Scott's 'Ben Ghoil, the Mountain of the Wind'. The wild and beautiful island, lying on the west of the Firth of Clyde, is some twenty miles long and ten miles wide — the largest island in the Clyde estuary. Goat Fell is the highest peak in the island, although there are several over 2,500 ft. The village of Brodick lies to the east of the pier, and almost a mile and a half beyond is Brodick Castle, a modern mansion in the Scottish baronial style.

42. DUNDONNELL FOREST, ROSS AND CROMARTY

Dundonnell Forest looks most attractive in the spring, with the fresh green leaves and purple heather. Covering an area of some 25,000 acres, the Forest lies at the head of Little Loch Broom, about six miles south of Ullapool, an attractive little fishing town in north-west Ross and Cromarty. The mountain in the background of this picture is An Teallach — a great hill of red sandstone with two peaks (3,483 ft. and 3,474 ft.), closely surrounded by lesser peaks.

43. DURHAM CATHEDRAL

The stately building of Durham Cathedral, set high on a rocky peninsula almost surrounded by the river Wear, makes a fine picture. It was on this site, in the year 995, that the monks of Lindisfarne rested the body of St Cuthbert, and the cathedral, begun in 1092, housed a Benedictine monastery until 1540. With its massive Norman nave and late Norman Galilee chapel — which contains the tomb of the Venerable Bede — it is one of the most beautiful examples of Norman architecture in the country.

44. THE WINDSWEPT MOORS OF WHERNSIDE

Whernside and Ingleborough, two of the great peaks of the West Riding of Yorkshire, flank the valley of the Ribble to the west, with Penyghent to the east. The dales and fells are always extremely popular among walkers, for the flat-topped mountains — all over 2,000 feet — are easy to climb, giving splendid views of the beautiful contours of the land. The soil over the rock is very shallow and in many places the limestone breaks through, giving a rather rugged appearance.

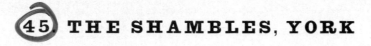 THE SHAMBLES, YORK

The Shambles, in the centre of York, is perhaps the most famous of a number of narrow, crooked streets in this city which survive from medieval days; it has been a butcher's street for a thousand years. Half-timbered houses such as these were erected at a time when land within the city walls was expensive. A big house could only be built on a small site by using the ground floor for business and having the first floor bracketed out to overhang the pavement. This was possible with half-timbered houses and is thought to be the reason why this type of house was erected instead of use being made of the beautiful magnesium limestone which was easily and cheaply available from Tadcaster, only nine miles south-west of York.

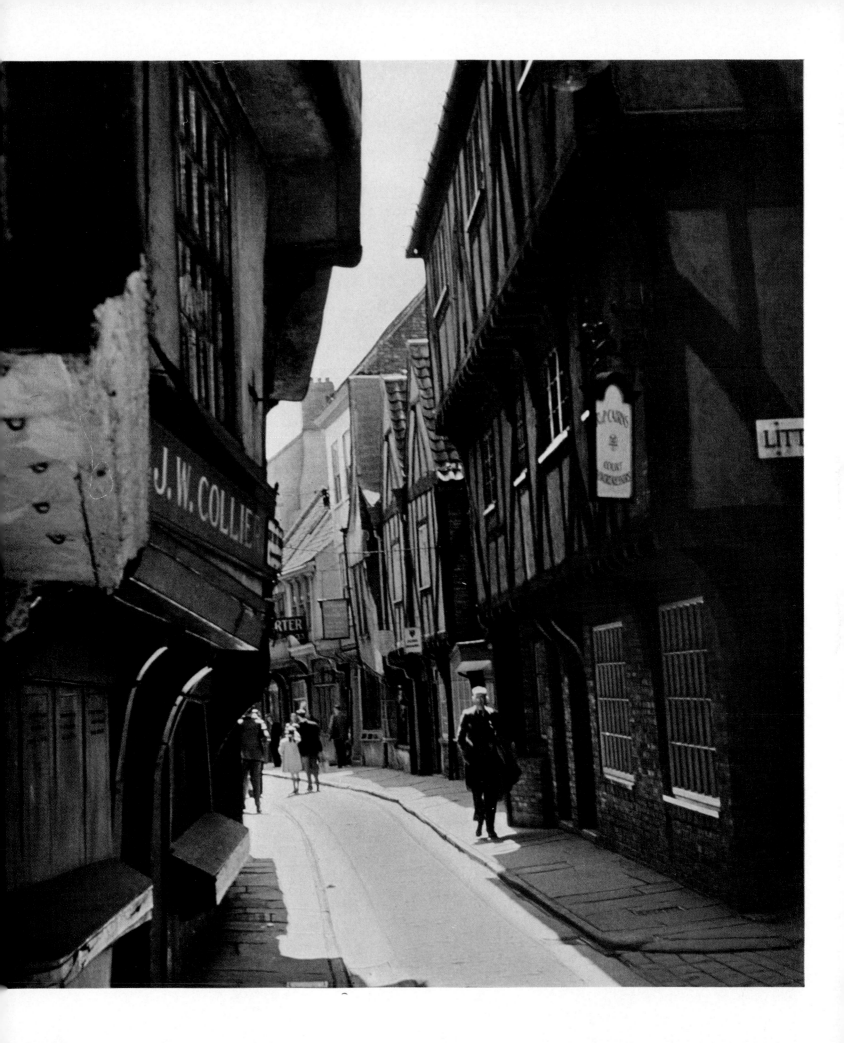

46. A TULIP FIELD
NEAR SPALDING

Every year in the Spring, countless visitors go to Lincolnshire to see the masses of brilliantly coloured bulbs which carpet the fields. There are more than a thousand growers cultivating some 2,200 acres of this fertile area in south Lincolnshire known as Holland, which is world famous for its thousands of tulips, daffodils and narcissi. This picture was taken near Spalding, one of the oldest market towns in the county, and famous as a centre for the cultivation of sugar beet, potatoes and bulbs. The river Welland, which runs through the town, is navigable for small sea-going craft and barges.

47. NORWICH CATHEDRAL

This famous Norman Cathedral stands in a loop made by the river Wensum, across which this picture was taken. The foundations were laid in the year 1096, in the reign of William Rufus, and building continued until nearly the end of the fifteenth century. The spire is of this later period; it rises from a much earlier tower to a height of 312 ft., making it, after Salisbury (404 ft.), the second loftiest in England. Norwich, Norfolk's capital, is a town of great historic interest. Its ancient grammar school had among its pupils the future Admiral Nelson, George Borrow and 'Rajah' Brooke of Sarawak.

48. HOUGHTON VILLAGE, HUNTINGDONSHIRE

These delightful little cottages, with their well-kept gardens, make an attractive picture. Houghton, on the river Ouse, is one of several pleasant villages in the county of Huntingdonshire; it lies about two and a half miles north-east of St Ives, an old market town which ascribes its foundation to St Ivo, a Persian missionary-bishop of the sixth century. Huntingdonshire, bordered by Northamptonshire, Bedfordshire and Cambridge-shire, forms a boundary between the Midlands and East Anglia.

49. TRINITY COLLEGE, CAMBRIDGE

The Great Court of Trinity is by far the largest and most famous of all the college courts.   Over the archway on the inner side of the massive Great Gateway may be seen the statues of James I, his Queen, Anne of Denmark, and his son, Charles I.   Trinity College owes its origin (in 1546) to Henry VIII, who incorporated several earlier foundations going back to 1317.   Rising from the carpet of forget-me-nots in the foreground of this picture, one can see part of the beautiful fountain erected by Thomas Nevile, Master from 1593 to 1615.   In the Chapel there are a host of fine memorials, including statues of Francis Bacon, Lord Tennyson and Sir Isaac Newton, all of whom were at the college.

50. FLATFORD MILL, SUFFOLK

John Constable, the famous landscape painter, was born at East Bergholt, a small village about nine miles south-west of Ipswich on the river Stour. His father, Golding Constable, owned several mills, including Flatford Mill, and John worked as a miller for a year before his father yielded to his passion for art. Flatford Mill became one of his favourite subjects and, like all the lovely country on the banks of the Stour, was immortalised by his paintings. The Mill, together with Willy Lott's Cottage, was presented to the nation in 1928 as an artists' hostel and studio.

51. EPPING FOREST

Epping Forest forms part of the ancient Waltham Forest which covered the greater part of the county of Essex—from Bow almost to Cambridge and thence to Colchester. The Forest became one of the royal hunting-grounds variously called Waltham and Hainault forests. It was threatened with total disafforestation, until under the Epping Forest Act of 1871 a board of commissioners was appointed for the better management of the lands. In 1882 5,600 acres were taken over by the Corporation of the City of London and dedicated by Queen Victoria to 'the free use of the London people for ever'. Epping, seventeen miles north-east of London, was once only a small market town with a wide main street. It has grown partly as a dormitory for London workers and partly as a recreational centre. This fine autumn scene was taken by the Wake Valley Pond.

52. THE ESSEX VILLAGE OF THAXTED

Thaxted, a medieval woollen market town with thatched cottages and a fifteenth-century Guildhall, lies seven miles north of Dunmow. It is well-known for its beautiful thirteenth-century church whose spire, 181 ft. in height, stands like a beacon above the village. This church has often been called the 'cathedral of Essex' and is much associated with the name of Conrad Noel, nicknamed 'the red priest', who was its vicar from 1910 to 1942. To the west of Thaxted lie the 'fields' — Finchingfield, Great and Little Bardfield, Toppesfield, Wethersfield and Gosfield. The picturesquely dressed foreign country dancers pictured here were taking part in a folk-dance festival.